OVERTHINKING

How to Declutter Your Mind, Remove Anxiety and Negative Thoughts, and Improve Your Social and Working Life.

PHILIP MORALES

TABLE OF CONTENTS

INTRODUCTION

O
verthinking (as the name implies) is excessive thinking about something, such as a subject, an issue, an event, or other matters, and what decisions to make regarding these subjects, issues, events, or other matters in the present or the future. Overthinking is not a behavior that only a few people exhibit; it happens to everyone in their daily lives. Maybe you have found yourself in a grocery store trying to select healthy food to purchase, spending way too long trying to decide which type of bread or tea that you would like to buy. Overthinking could also occur, for example, when we are playing a softball game, and our brain keeps planning, strategizing, and preparing when the ball has already been played by our opponent.

Some people experience constant overthinking; for others, this behavior occurs much less frequently. Research on overthinking has revealed that the brain constantly predicts the future and is always in anticipation of what will happen next. In a "Caveman Times" article, this behavior of the brain is compared to a caveman's prediction that a lion was probably following the heard of running antelopes, and he should stay away. But today, this can be compared to be mulling over the healthfulness of the meal items in a restaurant menu before selecting what to eat or drink. This could also mean carefully spending a lot of time considering the wording of a post to Facebook or Twitter while in fearful anticipation of harsh or critical judgment by the hundreds of followers and other people viewing the post.

Lori Hilt, Ph.D., an Assistant Professor of Psychology at Lawrence University in Wisconsin further explains that what happens to the brain when you over think is that you go round and round in a loop of repetitive thoughts when you ought to conclude on a course of action, move forward and solve the problem. While it is true that some degree of reflection helped us to survive and thrive in the past but too much also traps us in the realm of overthinking. Also, our past experiences and decisions are major contributors to our present overthinking behaviors.

Researchers have revealed that women tend to do more overthinking than men. At least about 42 percent of women excessively think about subjects, issues or events as a result of being too attuned to emotions while trying hard to understand them. This research then suggested that environmental factors such as how one is raised could contribute to this and that, furthermore, overly-controlling parents could be the cause because such mothers and fathers constantly suppress the thoughts of their kids.

According to Hilt, "Overthinking means we spend most of our time in the past or the future". Hilt says it is very hard to be in the present moment because the mind is constantly racing. One example of living in the past is a veteran soldier who comes back from a long war; he may try to deal with the present people in his life based on his interactions with other people during his war experiences. He may have found these people to be unkind, brutal or wicked; however, the people in his present life may or may not possess those certain characteristics. This war experience may cause the veteran to always think obsessively about what type of behavior to expect from them, what they mean, how to deal with them, etc.

The anticipation of the future is a type of overthinking that a student who is about to prepare for an exam might experience; he keeps thinking about the short time he or she has to read, what questions will be asked, or in what the instructor or examiner will mark his or her answer. Should he/she look at past questions or example questions? Will the results of this exam help or hurt his/her final grade? When, in reality, the best course of action for this student is to pick up the book and study.

Roy Baumeister, Ph.D., a research psychologist at Florida State University, who is also a co-author of the book called "Willpower", said that you tend to experience decision fatigue when you are trying to choose what to buy and not to buy, what to eat and what not to eat, or whether to go the gym or take a nap. All this lessens your self-control. He further makes his statement clear by adding that "you order a pizza because you are already overwhelmed to think about what to prepare for dinner, and it could be that you buy expensive appliances because you are worried out by making a comparison when shopping."

Domina Petric, MD, made it known that overthinking is a representation of a loop of unproductive thoughts. It is also considered to be an excessive amount of thoughts that are unnecessary. He further explained that overthinking can be linked to anxiety. In his approach to solve this overthinking disorder, he postulated that the entanglement of knots of negative emotions is expedient and should be replaced with positive knots of emotions.

Anxiety and depression can be the cause of negative emotions. In a situation where we can't find a balance between positive and negative emotions, negative emotions may take over. However, it is also important to realize that negative emotion is inevitable as it has its function in the balancing of healthy emotions. The ingredients of negative emotions are guilt, shame or disgrace, depression, despair, hopelessness, fear, worry, concern, nervous, irritation, frustration, annoyance, rage, panic, and more. These negative emotions happen naturally.

A person could be angered in a dangerous situation, and aggression has an important role to play by triggering the fast and efficient reaction to the dangerous situation; however, when the dangerous situation is gone, there is the need for positive emotion, such as gratitude, to balance the negative one. However, in a situation where such danger happens and is solved with anger or aggression, but there is no positive emotion to balance things, pathological anxiety and depression can occur. Knots of negative emotion lead to overthinking, and the mind can play a role in compensating this defection with intellectual overbalance.

Many factors lead to overthinking, such as excessive parental control, environmental factors during childhood, experience, emotional entanglement, and many more. This book will help you to discover how to stop and take action.

CHAPTER 1
SYMPTOMS OF OVERTHINKING

How do we discern that our thoughts are overthinking and not constructive thinking? How do we know for sure that we are overthinking? Well, there are some principles to follow. The purpose here is to detect, discern and determine if you have an overthinking disorder or not. Is an overthinking disorder just another form of anxiety?

Overthinking starts harmlessly as a normal way of reasoning about something, but it becomes harmful when it becomes a repetitive thought loop with no resulting action, leading to unproductiveness and frustration or depression.

Overthinking happens to everyone at a particular point or stage in life. To some, it happens seldomly, and to others, it happens with an alarming frequency. Have you ever found yourself obsessing over something or situation that it seems you can't control but keeps coming your way? Does it feel as if you don't have power over your mind anymore? You are overthinking instead of finding a solution and taking an appropriate course of action.

Overthinking is a result of some anxiety disorders. There are many different types of anxiety disorders that make an individual engage in overthinking or rumination. These disorders could be in the form of PTSD, Post Traumatic Worry Disorder, trauma, panic disorder, social anxiety, or agoraphobia. They could also be a result of some kind of illness, or they could also be substance-induced. Overthinking is a symptom of all of the above disorders.

An important thing to understand is that overthinking can't be experienced in the same way by two more people. But those that experience it will always discover that their life is being compromised by their inability to control their negative thoughts and emotion. This could lead to an inability to socialize, enjoy hobbies, and be productive at work because their minds spend a large amount of time on specific lines of thought, and this can also lead to mental health issues.

If you are the type that overthinks, you will discover that making friends or keeping them can be difficult to achieve because you may find it difficult to communicate with them about something that goes wrong, or you may communicate excessively with them. Besides, you can find it difficult to talk with other people because you are more concerned about what to say to them or what to do with them when you are in anticipation of what will happen. People who overthink may find it difficult to have a general conversation with people or to interact in a normal environment. Going to a store or an appointment may seem very hard, and they may struggle to do so.

Other behaviors that indicate that you are overthinking include:

- Being obsessed with what you should have said or done.

- Worry about how your co-workers perceive and judge your job performance

- Constantly engaging in "what ifs" about imaginary events that you fear could happen in a variety of circumstances.

- The aspect of catastrophizing, which is thinking of the worst scenario that may occur

- Being worried about unexpectedly having a panic attack

- Intrusive and obsessive thinking

INSOMNIA OVERTHINKING

Insomnia is the lack of ability to sleep. It is a sleeping disorder that is characterized by difficulty falling and staying asleep. People with insomnia may have one or some of the symptoms below, such as:

- Struggling to fall asleep.

- Waking up during the night but having trouble going back to sleep

- Waking up too early in the morning

- Feeling tired when they wake up

Insomnia can be divided into two categories: primary and secondary insomnia. Primary insomnia is a sleeping problem that does not relate to or is not directly associated with any other health issues or conditions. Secondary insomnia is a sleeping disorder that is caused by some other health-related issues, such as asthma, depression, arthritis, cancer, heartburn, and medications or other substances, such as alcohol. Additionally, insomnia can be acute or chronic. Acute insomnia may occur briefly, whereas chronic insomnia may last for a long time.

It is crucial to understand what insomnia is in order to understand why we can be obsessed with it. Overthinking can be a result of insomnia, and this can affect our quality of life because of the obsession with this issue (INSOMNIA) that we can't control. An insomnia patient's mind can race, and he/she can also be having obsessive thoughts about getting sleep. This is often as a result of the last occurrence of insomnia. Then it continues the next day and the next. This individual may feel tired, and his or her brain is less focused when occupied with a thought about not being able to sleep.

The reason why insomnia is a vicious circle is that when you have it, you will not be able to stop overthinking about not sleeping. About 90 percent of people with insomnia experience overthinking. It is always advisable to tackle the underlying causes of a problem in order to solve it more effectively. Overthinking that is related to insomnia needs medical attention, and this medical attention can lead to the reduction of having to over think or ruminate about it. Besides, overthinking could also make it worse for an individual with insomnia, which can turn into another kind of health-related issue. However, proper care must be taken to reduce overthinking for the individual with insomnia to prevent it from getting worse.

DECISION-MAKING ANXIETY AND OVERTHINKING

At one point or another, you may feel anxious about the decision that you are about to make. Decision-making is very important for every individual because it deals with making either the wrong choice or the right one. This puts a lot of pressure on the individual who is making the decision. Decision-making is another reason why people experience overthinking. Overthinking may occur when the decision is big, such as deciding which house to buy, or when it is small, such as picking an item for lunch at the restaurant.

According to Wikipedia, decision-making is the cognitive process that results in the selection of a belief or course of action among several alternative possibilities. Decision-making is also the step-by-step method of identifying and choosing alternatives based on the value, preferences, and beliefs of the decision-maker. These decisions often result in a final choice, which may or may not require any action.

However, human decision-making has been split into

three parts: psychology, cognitive and normative. The psychology aspect deals with people who make decisions based on sets of needs, preferences, and values the individuals have or seek while the cognitive aspect relies on a continuous process, and its integration is based on the interaction with his or her environment. It is also important to understand that all three are essential to solving problems, analyzing and making decisions.

Decision-making can be rational or irrational. This is through an economy where an individual is meant to make a decision based on this phenomenon. It is said that if a human can choose freely, he/she will make a choice that leads to the best situation for him/her while taking all the necessary considerations into account. These imply cost and benefit as well, and this could be termed as rational decision-making. However, this does not make a person's decisions unquestionable.

The rationality of decision-making can be questioned because of the contradictions that may occur during the process. These contradictions are factors that may prevent the decision-maker from making the right decision. One example is the challenge of making the right decision when faced with the same situation but framed in different ways.

ANXIETY INTERFERENCE

Since decision-making happens every day in human life, anxiety may occur based on the circumstances or situations related to a subject matter or issue. When it is there, anxiety tends to make people go the direction of the safest option for themselves, thereby leading them astray. It is not necessarily wrong to make a decision based on caution; it is sometimes the best direction to take.

Research published in the Journal of Neuroscience revealed how anxiety works to disengage the part of the brain that is essential for making the right decisions. This is called the pre-frontal cortex (PFC), and it is the area that brings flexibility into decision-making. What is the function of the PFC? It is the part of the brain that deals with planning, the weighing of consequences, and processing thoughts logically and in rational form. It also helps to take out the emotional steam from decision-making and helps to calm down the amygdala, which is the aspect of the brain that runs the instinct, impulse, and emotion.

The research further revealed that anxiety helped to reinforce good decision-making by reducing the capacity of the brain to eliminate distractions. While distractions can be physical things seen in our environment, they can also take the form of thought and worries. Anxiety interrupts the brain capacity to ignore distractions by numbing the group of neurons in the pre-frontal cortex, which is specifically designed to make choices.

OVERTHINKING COMES WITH ANXIETY

Anxiety negatively affects the brain's ability to make

choices with logical and rational reasoning. Overthinking could result in a variety of fears, such as the fear of accidentally making the wrong choice. This happens to leaders, celebrities, high-profile personalities, individuals, and role models. Making the wrong choice could have high-profile negative implications, and it puts a great burden on the individual making a choice based on the cost and consequences.

The criticism of a choice being made is sometimes a high price to pay for the individuals who must make these choices and occurs when people deem a decision as wrong, insane, forbidden or foolish. It has been the norm for some people to criticize others in a way that is not constructive. These people seek not to improve but to raise their self-respect at the cost or expense of others. They find faults and also lash out at the imperfection of others. And by so doing, they try to establish their dominance or superiority. For example, in the professional or academic sector, it is often seen in seminars or conferences, where professionals often pick out petty errors in others' reasoning or analysis for no good reason than just to look good in front of the audience. This poses great harm. For this reason, many find it as a struggle to make the right choice that won't bring about criticism, and this causes them to over think or ruminate over and over without action.

Wrong choices and past consequences are also other factors affecting the ability to make the right decision; these can lead to imperfect forecasting of results due to the recent decision that resulted in negative consequences for us. The experience of negative consequences should be to guide the decision-maker on the right path but could be an overwhelming factor that leads to overthinking and ruminating. This hesitation leads to no action and an unproductive result or failure.

Lack of confidence and demands from other people, such as subordinates or family, are environmental factors that can cause overthinking. The family could add the burden of their expectations to an individual who is trying to make the best decision for himself or herself. For example, a parent's may desire that a child finish well in college and get a good job; while the child believes he can excel without going to school in his football career but has to decide what should do in case he/she fails to succeed in what he/she is passionate about doing. As a result, schooling will be unproductive, and passion will also yield no results. Failure, then, will be uncontrollable, and obsession about failure is inevitable.

BIPOLAR DISORDER AND OVERTHINKING

Bipolar disorder is a health problem that was formally called manic depression. The health condition causes extreme mood swings for the individual having it; these include emotional highs and lows. When an individual is depressed, he or she may feel sad or hopeless and, as a result, may lose interest in most activities. If an individual's mood shifts to either mania or hypomania, such an individual may feel full of energy, euphoric, or irritated. Such mood swings may affect his or her sleep, energy, judgment, behavioral pattern, and his or her ability to think clearly.

While this poses a serious issue to such an individual, he or she may experience such episodes of mood swings rarely or multiple times in one year. Also, some people may experience emotional symptoms, while others may not.

This seems to be a lifelong health condition and can only be managed by medications and psychological counseling.

WHERE OVERTHINKING COMES IN

Since this is a lifelong issue, many people with bipolar disorder are also exposed to overthinking because their condition can lead to them being depressed or manic. As a result of having a hard time managing their emotional state, they may also experience overthinking.

In both the depressed and manic states of an individual with bipolar disorder, overthinking can upset or worry them. With depression, he or she may worry about what is going to happen next or in the future. Furthermore, he or she may be worried about the side effects of his or her medication.

An individual who experiences mania may have trouble focusing or paying attention to his or her thoughts; this makes it difficult for such a person to challenge his or her thoughts. It can be very hard to separate real life from fiction. Some often indulge in what they feel could make them safe and, later on, regret their actions.

Some bipolar episodes can last for a very long period, and overthinking can make it worse. It is, however, advised to seek the help of a medical practitioner to prevent such occurrences.

HYPOCHRONDIA

An individual with hypochondria may be physically healthy but will not stop going from doctor to another scheduling meetings and appointments, even when the doctor tells him or her that she is fine. They may still fear and feel that they are sick and always seek help to cure what they feel is wrong with them. Some may go as far as consulting Dr. Google for symptoms and take the result to their doctor, who will then tell them that there is nothing wrong with them.

SEEK MOTIVATIONAL RESOURCES

Although many individuals are skeptical about the value of motivational speakers, these motivational speakers are quite capable of helping them. Gaining information about another individual who has been able to overcome his or her anxiety and live through it, even sometimes at an older age, can encourage you and is a great way to distract you from your overthinking.

Seeking motivational resources is an excellent way to obtain mental health information that can be applied to oneself at a personal level. Although some of this information might not qualify as contemporary psychology, it is well worth researching.

Mindfulness is essential to getting the help you need. It is of great importance to examine all the health facts you may get about mindfulness. Some books are brief and don't take a whole lot of time to read. Others do take loads of time, but the facts they give are worth it. While some self-help books may look tacky, you'll be amazed at how much helpful advice about recuperation, rejection, guilt, failure, and problems that you can glean from them. In order to prevent overthinking, it's critical to read all the mindfulness books that you can.

GETTING HELP FOR AN ANXIETY DISORDER

Anxiety is a normal response to an adverse situation or event. If you think that you have an anxiety disorder or a cherished one has, you should not hesitate to get help. You should visit a therapist. An anxiety disorder is also related to depression, bipolar and other health issues that are associated with overthinking.

EXERCISE

Practice mindfulness thoughts through meditation.

If you can't fall asleep, always get out of bed and do something relaxing. You may also perform some exercise.

Split your goals into smaller ones and execute them one by

one.

Determine the cause of your anxiety.

Try noticing when you start to experience anxiety and use a variety of techniques to deal with it quickly and efficiently.

Always try to replace negative thoughts with positive ones.

Practice cognitive behavioral therapy.

Keep a list of your problems and try to solve them from the lowest to the highest priority.

Always avoid procrastination.

These are excellent strategies to stop overthinking. It is very important not to overlook any of these strategies as they will boost your brain's pre-frontal cortex (PFC) and also improve your mental health.

Overthinking can't be present without a root cause, and these roots causes are the underlying problems that trigger overthinking. Furthermore, they are also health issues that need the help of a therapist or a health practitioner. Some of these health issues that trigger overthinking have been covered here. We will now explore other causes of overthinking, their growth, and how they relate to an individual's feelings, mind and body.

CHAPTER 2
EMOTIONAL ENTANGLEMENT

Research on emotion entails constant and endless study into human nature. Emotions flow from an individual's mental state, which is directly associated with the nervous system, which undergoes chemical changes that are associated with thoughts, pleasure and displeasure, behavioral response or emotions. At the moment, there has been no scientifically agreed-upon single definition. The word emotion has often been used interchangeably with mood, temperament, personality, motivation, and disposition.

Various research studies from different fields have contributed to the study of emotion over the past two decades, and recently, the research on emotion has increased. Such research fields include psychology, medicine, history, sociology of emotion, endocrinology, computer science, and neuroscience.

Numerous attempts have been made, based on theories, to

reveal the origin, the neurobiology, and the experience of emotions, and these attempts have only led to more research into its sphere. Currently, the most popular area of research is the development of materials that stimulate and elicit emotion.

Wikipedia defines emotion as a positive or negative experience that is related to a particular pattern of physiological activity. Its production includes different physiological, behavioral and cognitive changes. Further research has revealed that the original function of emotions was to motivate such adaptive behaviors that would (in the past) have contributed to the passing on of genes through survival, reproduction and kin selection.

Understanding emotion is paramount to the subject of overthinking since emotion is dynamic and can take many different forms, such as positive and negative emotional knots. Overthinking involves an imbalance of emotion, or rather, emotional entrapment.

There are two types of emotional knots: negative and positive. While positive emotional knots are related to things that are positive such as love, joy, peace, and many more, the negative emotional knot deals with emotions such as depression, anger, anxiety, and many more. However, the role of the negative emotion is sometimes positive because it can assist us during certain situations and events. For example, aggression is needed for survival during troubling or heroic moments.

Entanglement can be seen as a defined system; one of its quantum states cannot be described as a product of its own without considering others. Entanglement can be seen as an inseparable object; it can have distance and independence but also depend on others. These entanglements form like tiny pieces that spin and interact with each other. However, if one goes south, the other will go north—clockwise and counter clockwise, respectively. Emotional entanglement (knots) takes the form of a group of emotional roles in an entangled state. They became inseparable and yet independent; for instance, aggression is independent of satisfaction and depression. Yet, they seek each and complement each other, as aggression seeks to achieve a good result while depression occurs due to a bad result.

CHAPTER 3
NEGATIVE EMOTIONS

According to Pam (2013), Negative emotion can be defined as unpleasant or unhappy emotions that were triggered in an individual to express a negative effect, particularly towards a situation or another individual.

Here are a few basic emotions:

- Anger
- Happiness

- Disgust
- Sadness

- Fear
- Surprise

Additional emotions (later included as part of a more expansive view of emotion) were included by renowned psychologist Eckman:

- Amusement
- Contentment

- Contempt
- Embarrassment

- Guilt
- Pride
- Relief
- Satisfaction
- Sensory pleasure
- Shame

With this list of emotions, we can vividly see which emotions have been deemed negative, such as Guilt, Shame, Embarrassment, etc. However, it is not the negative emotions that affect our well-being; rather, it is the ways and manner in which we react to them that affects us and also helps to determine our health status.

Being stuck in negative emotions would increase one's body's production of worry hormones and cortisol. With this, the cognitive ability to solve a problem, and to be proactive, is depleted. Also, it can damage our immune system by making it susceptible to other forms of illness. It is important to note that chronic worry has been revealed to be linked to a shorter life span.

In another sphere of study, the researcher has begun to look into what could be the link between negative emotions and cancer. While delving in, researchers based their focus on anger as a negative emotion and its link to cancer. It was mentioned earlier that negative emotion has positive effects, but an individual's reaction to their emotions is what will make it them better or worse. Anger is a normal feeling, but whether it is healthy depends on how it being expressed or not expressed. It's the manner of this expression that may sometimes cause problems. Anger could be referred to as unhealthy anger when it is intense, prolonged, or repressed. Unhealthy anger has been linked to cancer. However, another study revealed that patients with cancer presented an extremely low score of anger in a tested environment, and they suggested that the patients were either repressing or suppressing their anger. Researchers then suggested that anger could be a precursor to the development of cancer.

Further evidence supports the claim about the link between anger and cancer. One statistic showed the positive relationship between the extreme repression of anger and breast cancer diagnoses. According to research, women repressing their anger showed an increase in levels of the serum Immunoglobulin A, and this has been linked to some autoimmune diseases.

IN WHAT CAPACITY CAN WE CONTROL OUR NEGATIVE EMOTIONS?

The possible best way of dealing with negative emotions is through acceptance. As there are benefits to negative emotions, compelling ourselves to be happy most of the time can similarly be ominous to our well-being.

Enduring adverse emotion in ourselves, and other individuals, empowers us to develop sympathy for how they may present themselves and empathy for why they may present themselves. Rather than getting stuck in a viewpoint that negative emotions ought to be avoided or that they are somehow 'wrong' to experience, we need to recognize they are essential elements of our character.

When we do that, we can genuinely begin to change how we may respond to them and create practices that are meaningful and help us to engage more positively with others.

CHAPTER 4
UNDERSTANDING AND MANAGING, PROCESSING,AND EMBRACING NEGATIVE EMOTIONS

As positive psychology has expanded our understanding of our negative emotions, it's similarly been able to outfit us with various strategies for modifying these emotions in our daily lives.

Sims (2017) examined ways to deal with negative emotions proactively by acknowledging negative emotions; he devised the contraction TEARS of HOPE to help coach and guide individuals, which is described below in greater detail.

T = Teach and Learn

This is the path toward checking out what your body is trying to tell you through the presentation of negative emotions; it is better to acknowledge what these emotions mean. This builds your one-of-a-kind understanding of the way you respond to emotional states by allowing you to decipher the sign your body is sending you and determine what purpose this emotion fills.

E = Express and Enable

Negative emotions urge us to express them. They are actionable emotions. This segment of the acronym urges you to explore your emotions with straightforwardness and curiosity. It's connected to increasing the acceptance of your instincts and enabling them to be accessible without scorn.

A= Accept and Become More Acquainted With

This element of the acronym allows you to become more acquainted with yourself and how you are as a human. Focus on increasing your acceptance through positive affirmations to bring your hover of negative emotions into a space of affirmation.

R = Re-Evaluate and Re-Layout

When you accept your emotions as part of your character, you can begin to focus on reframing the condition and how you react. Just because an antagonistic inclination has risen doesn't mean that you have to react in a way that will have negative effects on you and individuals around you.

Enduring antagonistic emotions isn't a way of maintaining, tolerating, or making excuses for poor habits or practices; it's a way of caring for oneself and improving our reactions to other individuals

S = Social Assistance

Understanding that negative emotions are accessible in every single one of us, and, for all intents and purposes, in a comparative way, can be a magnificent wellspring of compassion and sympathy to everybody around us. It's how we process our emotions that makes the difference, so watching someone in the throes of shock and understanding that they are essentially dealing with an obvious peril can encourage us to approach them with compassion, rather than shock ourselves.

H = Hedonic Success and Happiness

This is the route toward replacing our negative social experiences with positive ones. Since we, as a whole, are more likely to survey negative experiences immediately, it might be helpful for us to bundle them with positive experiences so that we don't fall into a ruminating trap. Consequently, we can focus more on assessing positive experiences.

O = Observe and Visit

Resist the urge to watch your reactions without ignoring them, suppressing them, or overly distorting them. Use care to convey your focus to your mind and body and what particular inclination that it is producing inside you. Deal with these reactions without judgment.

P = Physiology and Social Changes

As you watch your enthusiastic and mental responses, watch your physiological reactions, too. Focus on your breath, your heartbeat, and try to figure out the modifications in your physiology that a negative inclination may have caused. Resist the urge to judge these modifications in your physiology.

E = Eudaimonia

This presumably won't be a word you think about; anyway, it's well worth adding to your language. Eudaimonia is a Greek word that essentially implies having a better-than-average soul. It occurs when you have found a state of being that is merry, strong and prosperous, and you have made sense of how to partake in exercises that result in your general thriving. It means that you're successfully trying to feel that all that you do is meaningful and valid.

I've encountered the assessments available and, moreover, assembled the underlying tips to empower you to supervise and provide you with the methods to handle negative emotions and develop habits that will help you to understand them and motivate yourself to improve your emotional state.

EXERCISES

Practicing gratitude has been deemed to have marvellous effects for both the recipients and providers. These effects have along-lasting impact on our perspective on events and life in general.

Whether it's an easily-overlooked detail or a significant thing, telling someone face to face or by phone, a letter, or a text how much that you appreciate something that they have done, can genuinely impact the way that you see and respond to negative emotions.

Use the TEARS of HOPE course to understand why you may respond to events, individuals, or situations the way that you do. Self-care can empower you to find the headspace to do this positively.

Understand How to Respond, Rather Than React

Do you know the difference between how you respond versus how you react? Negative emotions, much of the time, encourage us to react quickly to a given circumstance. When we feel irate, we may lash out or holler. These negative reactions may have many drawbacks; we may, for example, repel the people around us.

By exploring your negative emotions, you can start to develop an awareness of when you are reacting negatively and adapt more positive strategies for responding —in some cases, this could mean realizing that no reaction (in any way, shape, or form) is required.

Acknowledge When to Take a Break.

Acknowledge when to take a day to yourself. If you are continually experiencing negative emotions and endeavouring to direct them, your body is revealing to you that something isn't right.

Take a day to re-center. Fill this day with positive experiences, achieving the things that you know fuel you and make you feel better. This kind of break can help you to realign your thinking, give you some space to refocus on why you may experience negative emotions, and devise some positive strategies for adjusting your behavior.

This is just a quick summary of the tips that I feel would be most valuable; some tips may work better for you than others. Everything comes down to you as an individual. Some of these tips may work genuinely well and others, not so much. Assess two or three different methods and find the ones that work best for you.

CHAPTER 5
CULTIVATE HEALTHY HABITS

Rethink Resolutions

The issue with resolutions is that they have a yearly expiration date. It's nonsensical to put a one-year limit on a practice that will deliver us a lifetime of health.

Several more research studies demonstrate that the way to excellent wellbeing is a term that specialists call "lifestyle medication" — rolling out improvements in diet, exercise, and stress management.

It doesn't matter if you are working in Corporate America or slaving ceaselessly as a full-time mother, it is very simple to fall into an undesirable way of life these days. Do you frequently end up feeling exhausted or disheartened? Have you always had the need to completely change yourself to improve things? However, are you uncertain about where to begin?

Fortunately, like your daily espresso or how you binge reruns of Orange Is the New Black, developing sound habits is as simple as arranging a meeting with a co-worker while shopping in the produce area of your local supermarket. In some cases, we all need a little push of inspiration.

How would we develop solid habits and roll out positive improvements in our lives? We have two choices: we can relinquish something that isn't working, or we can present something new that will.

For instance, we can stop (or seriously limit) our consumption of French fries, or we can focus on consistently eating an additional daily serving of veggies. This type of decision brings about a progressively nourishing diet.

It might be useful to quit unhealthy practices to remain balanced; we should replace them with healthier options, such as substituting a plate of mixed greens for French fries when eating out.

To be effective, we should make space for change by saving time and energy to take part in new practices. A lot of us are totally over-booked, living on autopilot and moving excitedly through the days and hours, taking part in similar exercises and thoughts and doing similar things again and again, even though they are not working.

One meaning of craziness is to continue doing what you are doing again and again while anticipating an alternate outcome. What number of us are doing only that, possibly without acknowledging it — eating the same unhealthy foods while wanting to get in shape or hoping to feel invigorated while never setting aside some time and effort to work out?

To transform our mentality, we initially need to see what isn't working or what we need to get rid of. At that point, we should intentionally focus on deduction and carrying on in an unexpected way. Focusing on every little detail and rolling out little improvements can help move us toward our most profound wants and needs. We don't have to overpower ourselves with a lot of modifications at the same time. Little changes can prompt huge outcomes after some time.

Every day is another chance to start once more, but we can gather momentum just by getting started. I urge you to start where you are. What do you need more of? What do you need less of? In what capacity will you start to develop it?

Harness that inspiration and start making dependable, amazing changes that will improve your psychological and physical wellbeing.

Approach these changes with strong, positive, continual intent, and dump the New Year's resolutions. This time stamped, brief pledges will simply help you, in the best-case scenario, to develop temporary positive results. Alternatively, use the power of the New Year to create strong intentions that you can reiterate once per day and maintain for a lifetime. The customized, repetitive, and solid nature of inclinations is the best approach to flourishing in the long-term. Everything considered, what we do daily matters more than what we do from time to time. Here are some keys to developing a more beneficial way of life for 2019 and beyond.

Start Again (Without Any Preparation)

We've dismissed the basic elements of strong living and put our trust in "cutting edge" and complex programs, ricocheting from one program to another. In any case, by what method may we work on the fundamentals if we haven't generally enabled them to accomplish something stunning? This year, maintain a strategic distance from these examples and stick with the tried and true.

Certified food is stimulating, sustaining, prevents disease, and boosts attitudes—all that we need to live a long, strong, and cheerful life. Fiber-rich whole grains, extraordinary proteins, and strong fats, for instance, nuts, seeds, olives, and avocado—all of these rich, whole foods are perfectly packaged with the supplements, minerals, fiber, cell fortifications, and other essential elements that we need to prosper. In any case, mulls over exhibiting a normal portion of our eating routine is included ultra-dealt with sustenance's that are without important enhancements just as contain unsafe and phony included substances.

Water: The human body is around 65-70% water, an undeniable indicator of its importance to human health. Water supports the essential activity of every organ in the body, from transporting food, regulating the body's temperature, repairing the tissue, detoxifying the body, etc. Sufficient water replenishment is essential to perfect health, yet research indicates that a striking 75% of Americans are working under a wearisome absence of hydration.

Rest: Sleep is simply our body's opportunity to fix, patch up, and restore, yet we are more occupied with our mobile phones than we are about our most critical device of all: our body! As to flourishing, rest is routinely under-recognized. Studies show that over 33% of the U.S masses are anxious. Rest is as equally important as sustenance for improving health. Believe it or not, rest influences what we want, what we eat, our supplement use, our worry hormones, our weight, our imperativeness level, our perspective, and our education level.

Improvement. Our bodies were created to move, to act, and to achieve our goals, yet consistently, we are becoming progressively stationary. Studies measure that American adults spend, on average, 13 hours sitting each day, and only20% meet the CDC's physical development rules. While it's true that you can't work off a habit of unhealthy eating, there are a many important reasons to move your body. Standard exercise advances rest quality, improves academic performance, improves processing, keeps weight down, redesigns physical presentations, and supports progressively valuable sustenance choices.

Breathe. Our masses are living under perpetual pressure, anyway really, the more that we take care of ourselves, the more we can ask of ourselves. "Unplugging" improves proficiency, imagination, health, and fulfillment. Whether it's yoga, reflection, reading a book, cleaning, drinking a cup of tea, or doing an enema, taking a break to loosen up and reset is essential to our health and satisfaction.

Recognize What Areas That We Need to Work on for Long-Term Wellbeing.

Most of us realize that we have to eat healthily, workout, get lots of rest, and drink heaps of water to lead a healthy lifestyle. Several individuals believe they are making a better than average effort to be healthy. Notwithstanding, a large portion of us are not. One examination found that only three percent of adults meet every one of the criteria to maintain a healthy lifestyle. According to scientists, there are four keys to healthy living, including:

- Not smoking.
- Maintaining a healthy weight (a BMI of 18-25) or effectively getting in shape to achieve this.

- Eating a minimum of five servings of vegetables and fruits daily.
- Exercising for a minimum of 30 minutes, five times each week.

Few of us really accomplish every one of these things. And although these are significant, there is a lot more to being healthy than meeting the criteria stated above. It's likewise about having a positive frame of mind, a positive mental self-image, achieving psychological wellness, and spending time with your loved ones. In this way, before you decide to work on self-improvement, select which areas you want to fortify. Start with what you need to work on most and work your way up.

Recognize What Works For You.

Your ability to lead a healthy way of life will rely upon formulating ideas/strategies that work with your character. Pause for a moment to think about the times that you have succeeded and the times that you have battled with things. What conditions were most useful to you and encouraged you to make your best effort?

What circumstances did you find diverting? What prevented you from working toward and achieving your objectives? Whatever your objectives are, before you can make changes to your way of life, you must realize where you're coming from and have an understanding of the reasons that you would like to make changes. Recognize what works for you and what doesn't.

Break Unhealthy Habits.

The things we do all the time, from brushing our teeth to eating certain snacks, regularly form our habits. The initial move toward changing any conduct is to assess our present habits.

If you're prone to practicing each morning, that is great. If you're prone to purchasing a pack of chips and a soft drink each evening that is definitely not. You must search for approaches to break that pattern and build up new patterns while proceeding with your healthy habits. Start rolling out little day-by-day improvements. Pack healthy foods to take to work. Carry a refillable water bottle with you so that you can remain hydrated for the duration of the day.

Modify Your Approach

While the five crucial segments to healthy living are deceivingly simple, they are often difficult to achieve. What we need is a detailed plan to truly implement these basics vigorously in our daily lives. Furthermore, we don't require just any plan; we need one that takes into account our individual qualities and tendencies. There is no one-size-fits-all formula for healthy living. Healthy living is achieved by finding the practices that work best for you. Here's how you can achieve a healthy lifestyle that works for you:

Become More Self-Aware

While the basics of healthy living are the same for all humankind, how we complete them will vary from person to person. Your ability to thrive will depend upon how well that you can find techniques that line up with your personality type and your individual characteristics. It's much less complex to change your methods to fit with your character than it is to endeavor to wedge yourself into an inflexible structure that goes again sty our nature.

Do you need duty, or do you challenge responsibilities?

Do you lean toward disengagement or social settings?

Do you lean toward consistency or variety?

Are you a night person or a morning person?

Which strategy do you prefer: coordinating or maintaining a strategic distance from someone/something?

Are you organized, or do you like to live carelessly?

Would you like to make enormous steps or small advances?

How you answer these questions will empower you to recognize the best frameworks for bringing back the essentials. For example, if you are someone that requires obligation, seeking regular exercise classes or finding an activity buddy may empower you to maintain a regular exercise plan. If you're someone that prefers variability, having a structured, detailed exercise plan may be troubling and stressful for you; perhaps a Class-Pass enlistment offering a variety of classes and a flexible schedule will keep you engaged.

Use Habit Hacks

Since you have now decided what habits you would like to form, you are ready to start forming them. Molding new habits can be as difficult as breaking old ones, but there are various methods and strategies that you can use to combat this. Here are a few helpful tips to help start you in the right direction:

Focus on every element of the habits that you would like to achieve and separate them into smaller, more manageable parts. This will shield you from feeling overwhelmed and compromised from trying to change too much, too soon, and it will reframe the inclination into a task so basic that it is simple to achieve. For example, if you drink ten glasses of water in a day, remind yourself to drink a huge glass of water every hour.

When a task is scheduled, it becomes necessary, encouraging us to manage our time around it. We can also obtain a sense of achievement from crossing tasks off our list when we are finished. Create an hourly event in your calendar to remind you to take a brief walk and grab a glass of water, and include your step-by-step activities in your schedule.

Redoing: Recreate your space to create the best environmental conditions for your success. Remove things from your space that trigger you to revert to unhealthy habits and replace them with things that aid you in developing healthy habits. For example, give your kitchen a makeover; place healthy food choices at eye level, and store less healthy food son the top row of your cabinet, out of arm's range. Assemble your duffel pack the night before an activity.

Make Room in Your Schedule for Both Work and Play

Numerous business visionaries guarantee that work–life balance is a legend. The act of creating balance in our lives frequently constrains us to make concessions. It feels like a giant balancing act, and we're overwhelmed with commitments and stress. To an ever-increasing extent, organizations understand that we have to address life matters while at work and that we need flexibility in our work routines.

The fact is, rather than concentrating on the limits where your work life ends and your individual life starts, search for approaches to mix a fulfilling and combination of both. Concentrate on making reliable, sound, positive decisions that mirror your qualities, duties and objectives over the course of your life.

Oversee pressure.

Our reality is that we live in profoundly dynamic and pressurized conditions. Our lives pass by so quickly that it's frequently a battle to keep up.

This puts a lot of pressure on us. It's essential that we recognize which things are within our locus of control and which things aren't. For instance, getting a punctured tire is not within your control, but getting a terrible audit for imperfect work is within your control.

You can decrease and manage your worry by assuming responsibility for the things that you can control. Then, when unforeseen upsetting occasions occur, you will be relaxed and focused enough to concentrate on and take care of those issues without becoming overpowered. You can likewise participate in relaxation techniques, for example, meditation and breathing deeply, to enable you to oversee feelings of stress.

Slow Down and Stay in the Moment.

Many of us are so focused on our occupations and regular undertakings that we neglect to appreciate the present moment.

Take a moment to slow down and appreciate your surroundings, such as the sound of giggling, how the sun feels all over, and how your legs feel as you walk. Make time for gratitude at several points in your day.

The business world is orderly and requires steady advancement and examination; you are only as good as your latest achievement. Figure out how to appreciate each step of this process. Doing so will add to your sense of achievement and will make the ultimate result considerably more satisfying.

A way of life ought to be something that supports your life objectives. Take a step back and ask yourself: What would you like to accomplish, get involved in, or create in your lifetime? How can you pursue your interests and desires and accomplish your life aspirations? Regardless of whether it's raising a family, venturing to the far corners of the planet, or beginning your very own organization, each aspiration turns out to be increasingly achievable when you accomplish wellbeing and prosperity.

CHAPTER 6
INTERRUPT THE WORRY HABIT

In a meeting, author and speaker Joanie Yoder shared her account of how stress almost destroyed her life—until she discovered the answer in a flash of brilliance.

"My life was full of tension and stress; however, I had the option to cover it up, as many individuals do, until I had an encounter that made me hit absolute bottom. It was then that I had to confront my tensions, my feelings of dread, my fear, and my stress.

"Catherine Marshall said that the best revelation we can make is to understand that we cannot do everything on our own; that our own qualities are insufficient. I came to that discovery on my own. I didn't have anything left of my own inward assets. I did not seem to have the ability, physically or inwardly, to go on.

"I had developed agoraphobia, which is a fear of open

spaces—a dread of going out. I most dreaded going to the grocery store. It was so serious that I would freeze and start perspiring. I was anxious about the possibility that I would go absolutely crazy in front of strangers—the feeling was beyond words.

"Here and there, I would leave the grocery store in the middle of shopping, push my truck into a corner, and run home. When I was in the house, I felt elation at being sheltered and secure once more.

"I thought that I was the only individual who felt like this. My dietary patterns changed, my rest was inconsistent, I was trembling and unstable, and I was constantly on edge about existence and every one of my duties. I couldn't confront anything. I only managed to deal with it when I was in my mid-thirties.

"There were reasons for my trouble. As I think back now, I understand that there were three explanations behind my powerlessness to oversee life:

"One was extraordinary adolescence. I was genuinely too immature to deal with my duties.

"Secondly, I had built up a propensity for sharpness. All things considered, I didn't generally realize it, although my motive was noble.

"What's more, the third reason, which I believe is normal fours all, was an inclination to act naturally adequate. I attempted to do everything on my own. What's more, even when I understood that I couldn't do it all alone, I believed I should have been able to.

"Those three components had a disintegrating impact. They drove me toward a breakdown that I required. I believe it's a breakdown that we, as a whole, need. It was everything but a mental meltdown; it was a breakdown of my independence.

"From my very own involvement, and furthermore, in watching other individuals who are in this agonizing circumstance of coming up short on their assets, one of the qualities is a need to control—the need to control life, conditions, individuals, and even God—since we feel terrified of what may occur. We feel that on the off chance that we can control things and cause things to go a specific way, we will be less apprehensive.

"My concern was that I didn't feel responsible for my self-assurance—insurance from the things that I feared. So I started to manufacture a wall around myself. That case progressed toward becoming as little as the word suggests. I had a minor space in which I had a sense of security and secure—the four dividers of my home. Truth be told, I so cased my life that it contained a populace of one—me."

Is it accurate to say that you are tormented by consistent stresses and restless contemplations?

Worries, doubts, and anxieties are a regular part of life.

It's entirely expected to worry over an unpaid bill, an exceptional imminent representative gathering, or a first date. In any case, "run of the mill" worry becomes pointless when it's consistent and runs wild. You worry every day over "vulnerabilities" and unlikely scenarios; you can't dump nervous considerations out of your head, and they interfere with your daily life.

We may not all relate to Joanie's strategy for adapting; however, we, as a whole, recognize what it is to confront circumstances that make us uneasy, even panicky. A few of us stress over occupational circumstances, wellbeing, or a family that is self-destructing. Stress can appear as throbbing cerebral pain. Others experience a beating heart and brevity of breath. For still others, unrecognized dread sneaks behind our propensity to indulge, overspend, or abuse whatever will stifle the torment. We all face conditions outside our ability to control.

Frequent worrying, negative thinking, and consistently expecting the worst to happen can contrarily influence your emotional and physical health. It can, as well, zap your emotional strength, leaving you feeling anxious and apprehensive, causing insomnia, headaches, stomach issues, and muscle weight, and make it difficult to concentrate at work or school. You may take your negative emotions out on the people closest to you, self-fix with alcohol or meds, or endeavor to involve yourself by wandering off in fantasy land before screens. Excessive worrying can similarly be a huge element of Generalized Anxiety Disorder (GAD), an anxiety issue that incorporates strain, fear, and unease that goes back as far as you can recall.

If you're tormented by exaggerated worry and tension, there are steps you can take to stop anxious thoughts. Endless worry is a mental habit that can be broken. You can train your mind to stay calm and look at life from a more logical perspective while avoiding catastrophic thinking.

For what reason is it so hard to stop worrying?

Constant worrying can bring about critical harm. It can keep you up at night and make you feel tense and anxious during the day. Also, regardless of whether you despise feeling like a nervous wreck, it can be so difficult to stop. For most unending worriers, the tense thoughts are fueled by the feelings—both negative and positive—that you hold about worrying:

You may have negative feelings about anxiety. You may acknowledge that your constant worrying is ruinous, that it will make you crazy or impact your physical health. Or then again, you may be anxious that you will lose all authority over your worrying—that it will never stop. Negative feelings, or struggling with worrying, adds to your anxiety and increases worry; positive feelings about worrying can be just as harmful.

You may have positive feelings about anxiety. You may feel that your worrying is keeping you safe from fearful things, neutralizing issues, setting you up for a solution, or helping you to make plans. Maybe your belief is that if you keep obsessing about an issue long enough, you'll eventually figure it out. Or then again, perhaps you're convinced that worrying is the ideal approach to promise yourself so you won't disregard something. It's difficult to get out from under the worrying penchant unless you acknowledge that your worrying fills a positive need. At the point when you comprehend that worrying is the issue, not the solution, you can then start to regain control of your worried mind.

EXERCISE TIP 1: CREATE A DAILY "WORRY" PERIOD

It's difficult to be effective in your step-by-step practices when anxiety and worry are governing your contemplations and preventing you from concentrating on your work, school, or your home life. This is where observing your thoughts can help. Rather than endeavoring to stop or discard a tense idea, permit yourself to have it, but put off ruminating about it until later.

Make a "worry period." Choose a set time and spot to be anxious. It should be consistently available (for instance, in the family room from 5:00 to 5:20 p.m.) and early enough that it won't make you nervous right before rest time. During your anxiety period, you're allowed to worry about whatever's at the front line of your contemplations. The rest of the day is a worry-free zone.

Record your anxieties. If an anxious thought or worry

comes into your head during the day, make a short note of it and, after that, continue about your day. Remind yourself that you'll have the chance to think about it later, so there's no convincing motivation to worry about it right now. Recording your insights—on a pad or your phone or PC—is much harder work than simply thinking them, so your worry will undoubtedly lose their ability.

Go over your "worry list" during the anxiety time period. If the worries that you recorded are upsetting you, make yourself worry over them, but only for the proportion of time you've allocated for your anxiety period. When you start to deal with your worries in this fashion, you'll consistently feel that it's easier to develop a more balanced perspective. Likewise, if your anxieties don't seem, by all accounts, to be critical anymore, you can cut anxiety period short and enjoy the rest of your day.

Tip 2: Challenge Restless Thoughts

If you experience the ill effects of interminable uneasiness and stress, the odds are that the way that you look at the world causes potential situations to appear more catastrophic than they really are. For instance, you may overestimate the likelihood that things will turn out unfavorably, bounce promptly to most pessimistic scenario situations, or treat each on-edge thought as though it were a certainty. You may likewise dishonor your own capacity to deal with life's issues, accepting that you'll self-destruct whenever there's any hint of an issue.

The most effective method to challenge these musings:

During your stress period, challenge your negative considerations by asking yourself:

- What's the proof that the idea is valid? That it's not valid?

- Is there an increasingly positive, practical method for taking a gander at the circumstance?

- What's the likelihood that what I'm terrified of will actually occur? If the likelihood is low, what are some other possible outcomes?

- Is this thought or idea useful? In what manner will agonizing over it help me, and in what capacity will it hurt me?

What would I say to a companion who felt this stress?

Tip 3: Distinguish Among Resolvable and Unsolvable Worries

Research shows that while you're worrying, you unexpectedly feel less nervous. Running over the issue in your brain helps you to manage your emotions because it causes you to feel that you're accomplishing something. Regardless, worrying and problem-solving are two very different things.

Problem-solving incorporates surveying a condition, creating strong steps for overseeing it, and a short time later, putting the plan in action. Worrying, on the other hand, only sporadically prompts plans. Despite how much time you spend imagining worst-case scenarios, you are not more prepared to deal with them if they should happen.

Is Your Anxiety Solvable?

Solvable worries are those you can deal with proactively right away. For example, if you're worried about your bills, you could call your loan specialist to consult him/her about your different options. Pointless, unsolvable worries are those for which there is no logically related course of action, such as worrying about the possibility of imminent disaster or envisioning a situation where your child gets into some sort of trouble.

If you are worrying about something that has a high probability of occurring, start conceptualizing. Review all the courses of action that you can take to resolve this potential problem. Take the necessary steps, but don't get too hung up on finding the perfect plan. Focus on the things that you can change, instead of the conditions or substances outside your locus of control. After you've surveyed your decision, decide on a course of action. At the point when you have a game plan and start dealing with the issue, you'll feel considerably less tense.

If the anxiety isn't actionable, recognize your helplessness. If you are a relentless worrier, most of your anxious contemplations will fall into this category. Focusing is often a possible away we endeavor to foresee what the future has in store; it is a way to deal with turn away loathsome astonishments and control the outcome. The issue is that it doesn't work. Considering all of the things in your life that could have negative outcomes won't make your life easier. Worrying about possible unlikely occurrences will simply prevent you from enjoying the many positive and helpful things that you have in the present. To stop worrying, give up your need for certainty and easy answers.

Do you, when all is said and done, catastrophically envision horrendous things will occur? What is the likelihood they will, in fact, occur?

Given that the likelihood is incredibly low, is it possible to live with the small probability that something negative may happen?

Ask your friends and family how they adjust to being able to prevent negative outcomes in similar conditions. Might you have the option to do so in like manner?

Tip 3: Talk About Your Anxieties

Talking very closely with a trusted partner or relative, someone who will listen to you without judging, denouncing, or becoming overly-involved is perhaps the best and calmest way to deal with what is occurring in your present reality and diffuse anxiety. When your anxieties start spiraling, talking them over can help you to feel validated.

Verbalizing your emotions can routinely help you to

make sense of what you're feeling and put things in perspective. If your fearful emotions are also outlandish, verbalizing them can reveal them for what they are—pointless worry. Likewise, if your worries are valid, describing them to someone else can help you to create strategies to solve them that you probably would not have thought of alone.

Build a strong support system. People are social creatures; we're not expected to live in disengagement. Regardless, a strong support system doesn't generally mean a large group of friends. Having two or three people whom you can trust and rely upon to be there for you has a number of benefits. Also, if you don't feel that you have anyone to trust in, it's never too late to assemble new friendships.

Acknowledge who to avoid when you're feeling fretful. Your fretful outlook on life may be something that you developed when you were growing up. If your mother is a relentless worrier, she isn't the best individual to call when you're feeling anxious—no matter how close you are. When pondering who to go to, ask yourself whether you will, by and large, feel significantly better or even more fearful after discussing your problem or issue with that person.

Tip 4: Interrupt the Stress Cycle

On the off chance that you stress unreasonably, it can appear as though negative thoughts are racing through your mind in a permanent loop. You may feel like you're spiraling wildly, going insane, or ready to break down from carrying the weight of this unease. Be that as it may, there are steps that you can take right now to eliminate those restless musings and give yourself a break from persistent stress.

Get up and get going. Exercise is a powerful enemy of worrying and unease since it discharges endorphins, which diminish strain and stress, help vitality, and improve your feeling of prosperity. Much more critically, by truly concentrating on how your body feels as you move, you can interfere with the steady progression of stressful thoughts going through your mind. Focus on the impression of your feet hitting the ground as you walk, run, or move, for instance, or the musicality of your breathing, or the feeling of the sun or wind on your skin.

Take a yoga or jujitsu class. By concentrating your psyche on your developments and breathing, rehearsing yoga or judo keeps your focus on the present moment, clearing your brain and leading to a casual state.

Reflect. Reflection works by changing your concentration from stressing over the future or choosing not to act on to what's happening at the present moment. By being completely occupied with the present moment, you can stop the endless loop of negative considerations and stress. Furthermore, you don't have to sit leg over leg, light candles or incense, or serenade. Basically, locate a calm, agreeable spot and pick one of the many free or modest cell phone apps that can guide you through the meditation.

Practice dynamic muscle unwinding. This can enable you to break the interminable circle of stressing by concentrating your psyche on your body rather than your considerations. By first tensing, and, on the other hand, releasing diverse muscle groups in your body, you release muscle pressure in your body. Furthermore, as your body unwinds, your mind will relax as well.

Attempt profound relaxation. At the point when you start to feel stressed, you become on edge and inhale more quickly, frequently prompting further uneasiness. Yet, by breathing deeply, you can quiet your brain and calm negative contemplations.

Tip 5: Observe Your Stressful Thoughts

Stress is generally caused when we focus excessively on the future—on what may occur and what we'll do about it—or on the past, rehashing the things that we've said or done over and over in our minds. You can break free from stressful patterns of thinking by returning your focus to the present. This technique involves watching your stressful thoughts, and, after that, releasing them. Observing your stressful thoughts helps you to recognize where your reasoning is causing issues and to reconnect with your feelings.

Recognize and observe your stressful thoughts. Try not to overlook, battle, or control them like you generally would. Rather, just watch them as though from an outsider's point of view, without responding or judging.

Release your stress. Notice that when you don't attempt to control the restless musings that spring up, they pass before long, similar to mists moving across the sky. It's only when you hold in your stressful thoughts that you will start to feel paralyzed by them

Remain focused on the present. Focus on how your body feels, the pace of your breathing, your constantly-evolving feelings, and the contemplations that float through your psyche. On the off chance that you end up ruminating about a specific idea, take your consideration back to the present moment.

Utilizing mindfulness to remain focused on the present is a basic idea; however, it requires some time investment and practice to receive the rewards. From the start, you'll most likely find that your mind will meander back to your stressful thoughts. Do whatever it takes not to become disappointed. Each time that you return your concentration back to the present, you're fortifying another psychological propensity that will enable you to break free of the negative stress cycle.

Do you believe that the Universe is working with you? When you can understand this, and realize that, regardless of what you experience, eventually, everything will be fine, you will never doubt that there is a being, more powerful than you, who is ensuring that everything will be fine.

Imagine how you need your life to be and, after that, allow the Universe to work with you, knowing and expecting that it will. This will greatly reduce your stress. By attempting to change your way of thinking, you achieve a more calm, relaxed, stress-free existence.

CHAPTER 7
OVERCOMING FEAR AND ANXIETY

Fear is one of our strongest emotions. It has an astoundingly strong effect on your mind and body.

Fear and anxiety can pop up for a brief period and pass only a moment later, but they can last much longer. From time to time, they can take over your life, affecting your ability to eat, rest, concentrate, travel, enjoy your day, leave the house, or excel at work or school. This can prevent you from achieving the things that you need to do or acquire the things that you need, and may, furthermore, impact your health.

Some people become overwhelmed by fear and the need to maintain a positive outlook about things that may make them startled or nervous. It will, in general, be hard to break this cycle. Be that as it may, there are multiple ways to do so. You will feel better if you learn healthy ways to deal with your fear; that way, you will not feel so overwhelmed by it that it doesn't keep you from living.

What makes you anxious or restless? Since anxiety is similar to fear, the strategies mentioned above also work well for anxiety. Anxiety occurs when fear is debilitating and endures over a prolonged period of time. It is connected to something that might or will happen in the future, rather than what's happening right now.

What do fear and anxiety feel like? When you feel frightened or nervous, your mind and body react quickly. Your heart may beat more quickly. You may breathe in extraordinarily fast, shallow breaths. Your muscles may feel weak. You may sweat a lot. Your stomach may feel queasy. You may find it difficult to concentrate on anything. You may feel frozen, cemented to the spot. You may not be able to eat. You may have hot and cold sweats. You may get dry mouth. You may get astoundingly tense muscles.

Over time, you may become depressed, experience trouble sleeping, develop headaches, have difficulty working and preparing for the future, have issues having sexual intercourse, and lose self-confidence.

These things happen because your body, detecting fear, is setting you up for an emergency, so it makes the blood in your body flow to your muscles and gives you the mental ability to focus on what your body sees as a threat. Furthermore, it may your elevate blood sugar.

Why do I feel like this when I'm in no real danger? Early humans required the fast, mind-blowing responses that fear causes because they were routinely exposed to physically dangerous conditions; regardless, we do not normally face comparable perils in modern-day living.

Regardless of this, our mind's bodies still work quite similarly to those of our early ancestors, and we have comparable reactions to our modern worries over bills, travel and social conditions. Nevertheless, we can't escape from or physically attack these issues!

The physical assessments of fear can be alarming in and of themselves – especially if you are experiencing them, and you don't have the foggiest idea why, or in case they seem, by all accounts, to be disproportionate to the situation. Instead of warning you about impending danger and setting you up to respond to it, your fear or anxiety can kick in when it perceives very dangerous or slightly dangerous. These situations could be imaginary or minor.

Why won't my fear go away? When will I feel normal again? A small amount of fear is normal when you are faced with something new. Or it could be a faint, slightly intuitive fear about someone or something, even though you can't put your finger on why. Some individuals feel constant fear and anxiety, with no particular trigger.

Understanding Panic Attacks

An anxiety or panic attack can be referred to as a time when you feel overwhelmed by feelings of fear and exhibit the signs mentioned earlier in this chapter. People who have attacks of nervousness often complain that they have difficulty breathing, and they worry that they're having a heart attack or will lose control of their bodies.

What is a Phobia/Fear?

A phobia is an over-the-top fear of a particular animal, thing, place or situation. People with fears have an amazing need to avoid any contact with a specific explanation behind the cause or fear. Coming into contact with the explanation behind the fear makes such a person with phobia fretful or panicky.

HOW CAN YOU HELP YOURSELF?

Face your fear if you can.

If you, by and large, avoid conditions that you are afraid of, you may stop achieving the things that you need or want to do. You won't have the chance to determine whether your fears regarding the situation are valid, so you may miss the opportunity to learn how to manage your fears and lessen your anxiety. As a result of being overly cautious, your anxiety may increase, Facing your fearful emotions and attacking the underlying causes can be a suitable technique for beating your anxiety.

Know Yourself

Get acquainted with your fear or anxiety. Keep an anxiety diary by jotting down your fearful and anxious thoughts when they occur. You can try setting yourself small, reachable goals for standing up to your fears. You can write down a list of things that you can look at now and again when you are most likely to become frightened or anxious. This can be a feasible technique for observing the beliefs that are behind your anxiety. Keep a record of when it happens and describe what happens.

Exercise

Exercise requires some concentration, and this can take your mind off your fear and anxiety.

Relaxation

Mastering relaxation techniques can help you to deal with the mental and physical feelings of fear. These techniques can help you to relax your shoulders and help you to improve your breathing. You may imagine yourself in a relaxing spot. You can also try alternative methods for relaxation, such as yoga, meditation, and back rubs.

Avoid Excessive Food Intake

Eat lots of fruit and vegetables, and avoid consuming too much sugar or sugary foods. Too much sugar consumption increases blood sugar; this can lead to feelings of tension. Try to go without drinking an excessive amount of tea and coffee, as caffeine can increase anxiety levels.

Avoid or Limit Your Consumption of Alcohol

It's normal for some people to drink when they feel

fearful. Some individuals call alcohol 'Dutch guts', yet alcohol can make you feel progressively anxious or tense.

Complementary Medications or Alternate Strategies

Some individuals find that complementary medications or exercises, for example, relaxation strategies, meditation, yoga, or tai chi, help them to deal with their anxiety. You can select whichever of these strategies that you prefer to win over your anxiety.

CHAPTER 8
THE LINK BETWEEN EXCESSIVE FANTASIZING AND OVERTHINKING

Which one interests you more? Fantasy or reality?

To begin with, we should look even more cautiously at the words "dream" and "reality." When an adult says that he/she understands the difference between dream and reality, how is she defining each word? By dream, he/she might infer fiction. As shownondictionary.com, "fiction" has a variety of suggestions. Fiction can mean a lie. When someone says that the media doesn't impact him/her since he/she understands the difference between dream and reality, I think he infers by "reality" that people and conditions on TV are made or composed. We know, for example, that the TV show Friends was a story about the associations and experiences of a social event of 20-year-olds. In what ways is the story fictional rather than true? Everything considered, adult observers realize that the people on T.V. are performers who are paid to play parts.

When we watch a TV show, we're essentially imagining that these are real people and these conditions and events are really happening as we watch them unfold. To the extent that we acknowledge these characters and their conditions and associations are possible and significant, we investigate them. To the extent that we become tied up with the fantasy, we are drawn into the show.

So where does reality come in, and what is the critical significance of "reality" in this particular circumstance? The reality of a recounted story isn't about whether it is a dream or a creation; it is about whether it is possible and could actually happen in real life. Paradoxically, the best kind of dreams are the ones that strike us, none way or another, as real or credible. We reflect on how much we would like to manifest incredible dreams in real life, and fiction is a representation of that very reality; it empowers us to envision a situation and to feel as though a particularly captivating or fulfilling story could be legitimate.

I once found two women looking at their dream darlings over coffee. They were discussing their favorite "celebs": celebrating their "hotness", what they love about them, why they would make bewildering darlings, and how amazing that it would be to meet them in person. Some time ago, on the news, I read a journalist's article about a pubescent youth asking a Sports Illustrated supermodel (who was probably his mom's age) to go with him to prom. He was admiring the young man's initiative and how he risked public humiliation to attract the woman of his dreams.

We live in a world where people imagine that they have fallen "in love" with T.V. and film stars, erotic entertainment stars, and supermodels. They are fascinated… from a distance. There is something about these fictional relationships that feel safe for these people. There is something that many people find engaging about connecting with famous people in their own darkened viewing rooms. (These fictional relationships can, of course, also occur in our real lives; people may fantasize about that individual at work that they have never truly chatted with.)Part of the allure is that they can safely (without consequence) project the characteristics and personality traits that they desire onto this person.

But somehow, maintaining a strategic distance from other people makes us need them altogether more. In any case, to really revere, as C.S. Lewis says, is to be unprotected.

However, this isn't just about crushing on Hollywood celebs; fantasy can infiltrate huge parts of our life. However, to dream is to live-in what isn't instead of living in what is. In this way, fantasizing can lead to overthinking: from suggestive amusement to destructive effects.

For example, a married man who constantly fantasizes about his young office secretary and constantly pictures himself in a relationship with her may neglect his own relationship. A single woman who becomes madly in love with a man who she's scarcely spoken with may imagine what their life could be like, choose names for their two children, or mentally furnish their dream house, only to have her heart broken by his disinterest. A housewife who is trapped in the fantasy and passion of her romance novels may surrender her own reality instead of working to improve it.

A young person who spends all his time fantasizing about his football career after he is forced to quit due to injury is escaping the present moment instead of pursuing equally fulfilling but more realistic career options. A miserable college student, surfing the internet for fantasy women, may avoid social opportunities that would permit him to connect with real-life women and experience fulfilling relationships.

Fantasizing about someone who is unattainable in real life may seem, by all accounts, to be a harmless indulgence, but it can lead people to infidelity and prevent people from pursuing meaningful, real relationships. These fantasies could also become a source of stress and inferiority as, by their very nature, our fantasies are unattainable; they could become a source of rumination and overthinking for someone who becomes anxious or depressed when real life does not meet their fantasy-fueled expectations. These expectations could also lead us to project certain qualities onto our prospective partners that are unrealistic and set ourselves up for perpetual disappointment.

Studies have exhibited that if you mix fact with fiction, people tend to be more likely to believe fake information. For example, in one assessment, German students read an episodic story called "The Kidnapping", into which either evident or false information had been implanted. A control group read an identical story without the announcements implanted. One certifiable insistence was that action fortifies one's heart and lungs. The counterfeit assertion was the opposite statement – that action weakens your heart and lungs. Results showed that the participants in the study were interested in the information that was provided to them but paid little regard to whether the information was true or false.

These researchers mulled over a phenomenon called the sleeper sway – the impact of recounted accounts augments after some time as the wellspring of the information dries up. What this investigation shows is that we can be inclined to believe false information that is implanted into a narrative story. Furthermore, after some time, we forget where we received this information and our trust in its reality increases...

The theory explaining why people are impacted by information in episodic stories is called transportation. People examining a book, watching a film or TV show, or playing a PC game become interested, engaged, or enthralled by the story; they may, furthermore, imagine that they have become characters in the story and that the experience is happening to them. This is one of the properties of the media that draws people in. When an episodic story transports us, we are open and uncritical because this process of transportation decreases our tendency to seek explanations, causes us to develop fictional relationships with the characters, and lends credibility to the story.

Our involvement in narratives such as these is not harmful in and of itself; however, excessive involvement in these narratives can, as previously mentioned in this chapter, be problematic when this fantasy supplements reality. In addition, this example illustrates just how unrealistic our life expectations may become, as the narratives we are presented with may sometimes be more fictional than factual.

For example, we may wonder why our love relationships don't resemble the ones that we see in the movies, which conveniently fit into ninety-minute time slots. We may worry that we have gone wrong somewhere, and this could lead to anxiety and overthinking. We may, for example, be an aspiring athlete who seems an Olympian's success and feels inadequate due to their own achievements; the T.V. program that we have just watched hasn't mentioned that this person may have had advantages that propelled their success, such as a hockey rink in their backyard.

While the allure of the fantasy is undeniable and fills an important place in our lives, if we become preoccupied to the point that we experience dissatisfaction, rumination, or excessive comparison of our lives with the lives of others, it can become just another cause of overthinking. It is important not to become consumed by fantasy; rather, use your dreams as fuel to create a better reality than the one in which you are currently living.

CHAPTER 9
STAYING POSITIVE

Let's be honest. Living, in and of itself, is a struggle. It can become difficult to deal with the realities of life. During these occasions, we are given only two choices: we can become a slave to our circumstances or rise above them. If we let our life circumstances rule our lives, we are forfeiting our futures. However, in the event that we can always see a silver lining, we will have faith that things that things will be better one day.

I realize that remaining positive is more difficult than one might expect. Be that as it may, even a minor dash of positivity will help bring us through life's difficulties. Try to consistently find something about your day to feel gratitude for; some days, you may need to look a bit harder than others.

Negative circumstances happen constantly. We can't keep away from them, so how might we neutralize their negative impact on our lives and our frames of mind? Learning about the power of positivity can help us to remain positive, even amidst catastrophe. Figuring out how to remain positive despite negative circumstances is essential to developing a stable life.

Researchers have discovered a multitude of advantages to remaining positive. Here are just some of their findings:

- Negative people had about a 20 percent higher mortality rate (over a 30-year time span) than the individuals who exhibited more positivity.

- People who found things to be grateful for once a week were more energetic and had less physical grievances than others.

- Conclusion: People who ruminate and focus negatively can achieve better mental and physical health by starting to focus more positively.

How to Bring Inspiration and Satisfaction Into Your Life

Keep a journal and, each day, write down a list of at least five things that you feel grateful for. Studies have shown that gratitude increases happiness, positivity, and life fulfillment. Read on further to discover more information on how to compose a gratitude list that works for you.

Listen to music that sounds how you want or need to feel. Research has demonstrated that music causes the cerebellum to discharge dopamine and, furthermore, relaxes the body. So "upbeat" music can make you feel more joyful!

Offer inspiration by sending one thank-you email or doing one kind act each day. There are several studies that demonstrate that acts of thoughtfulness can support satisfaction, diminish sadness, and even prolong your life.

Challenge your negative reasoning. Ask yourself: "Is there a more positive way in which I could view this situation?" Hundreds of studies have demonstrated that having the option to think hopefully is useful for your wellbeing and prosperity.

Be that as it may, it's not just about embracing a Pollyanna disposition—self-assured people are more effective problem-solvers and are better at tolerating terrible circumstances. Read further to figure out how to free yourself from negative thinking.

Grin. It may sound short-sighted; however, research has demonstrated that it really encourages you to feel more joyful. Facial muscles send a message to the cerebellum and improve our feelings; furthermore, it is much more likely that a grin is inspired by a positive idea. So grin at someone today; grin at your pet, or at a small child, or even your best friend.

Do something that you feel passionate about. Volunteer for a charity of your choice or take a class to gain some new useful knowledge. A few investigations have demonstrated that individuals who feel that their lives are meaningful achieve greater success, live longer and feel more fulfilled.

Meditate. Just seven minutes of daily meditation has been

proven to improve one's state of mind, decrease pressure, and improve sleep. Normal meditators concentrate better, are more emotionally stable, and experience more mindfulness.

Write down what your ideal future would look like if you met all of your objectives, and all of your dreams were fulfilled. To develop this idea further, write down a detailed account of your extraordinary future life. Writing your dreams down will help them to appear more real to you.

Set aside time to relax your mind and body. Analyst Laura King, Ph.D., an incredible state of mind promoter who demonstrated this activity, allotted 20 minutes on four successive days. A minor departure from this activity is to visualize positive results in especially dire circumstances.

- Search for the positive aspects that can be found in any situation. Searching for the silver lining in a negative circumstance may sound sappy; however, it can dramatically improve your quality of life. To locate your silver lining, ask yourself:
  - How has this circumstance caused me to grow?
  - Have I developed new abilities?
  - How am I glad about the manner in which I dealt with this circumstance?

Practice Gratitude

Seeing and valuing the positive parts of our lives can drastically improve our mindset and our ability to deal with adversity.

To build your thankfulness, you can:

- Write an appreciation letter. Specialist Martin Seligman, Ph.D., requested that subjects compose a letter expressing gratitude toward somebody who had been especially kind to them and, afterward, give it to them in person. The letter-essayists appreciated noteworthy constructive outcomes, even after a month.

- Keep an appreciation diary. Record anything, enormous or little, that makes you grin, including impressive accomplishments, material blessing, and amazing relationships.

- Remind yourself to enjoy life. Indeed, stop and take in all the pleasant things which life has to offer. Do whatever you can to truly absorb the lovelier parts of your life.

- Share your uplifting news. Studies of individuals' responses to positive life events recommend that individuals who tell a friend when fabulous things happen to them appreciate these things even more.

Let Go of Negative Thinking

If you need to feel positive, it pays to rid your life of negative people. With training, you can counter negative thoughts and turn your inner bully into a cheering squad.

Avoid focusing on negative aspects of your life, people, places, or things; this can make it harder for you to handle misfortune and trouble in your life. In a study of test-takers, the individuals who focused negatively performed worse than the individuals who were focusing positively. To adjust your focus:

- Ask yourself if the issue is really worth your time and energy. Will this issue matter in a year, for instance?

- Tell yourself that you'll stress over it at a designated time later. The odds are that you'll feel better by the designated time.

- Instead of ruminating unproductively, attempt to think critically, with a goal of resolving

- the issue.

- Distract yourself: See a film, listen to some music, and find something enjoyable to do.

- Stop the negative self-talk. You may have been running negative messages in your mind for quite a while. However, research demonstrates that you can change your way of thinking; you can actually change your mind. You can incorporate some elements of Cognitive Behavioral Therapy (CBT), which focuses on changing your life by eliminating negative, unproductive ways of thinking. A few hints include:

- Ask yourself if your negative idea is truly valid. It is safe to say that you are extremely a horrendous mother if you didn't make it to your child's class play? You've presumably made countless different decisions as a mother. It is unlikely that just one will define you.

- Reflect on any accomplishments that discredit your frailty. If you fear that you'll make a fool of yourself at the workplace party, recall other social events when you were active and sure of yourself.

- Imagine what you would tell a companion if he was stressing out in the same way that you are. You'd almost certainly persuade him to hold off on catastrophizing.

- Beware of win big or bust reasoning. Disillusioning your better half once doesn't mean that you're destined to frustrate her constantly.

- Consider getting all of the facts before you draw conclusions. Just because your manager has not approved your proposal does not mean that he doesn't like it; he/she could just be busy. You don't need to let bad news and negativity destroy your day. You have a decision about what you concentrate on and how you react to any circumstance. Incorporate these tips into your life, and I'm sure that you'll quickly perceive how the positives exceed the negatives.

CHAPTER 10
THE COURAGE TO TAKE ACTION

Your life would be better if you took the action that you've been avoiding. Maybe the biggest challenge that you will ever defeat in life is your tendency toward fear and dread; the prize will be the improvement of your mental strength and fortitude. Winston Churchill once stated, "Fearlessness is properly considered the first of ethics, for it is upon this that all others depend. "Fear is, and consistently has been, the best adversary of humanity. At the point when Franklin D. Roosevelt stated, "The main thing we need to fear is fear itself," he was stating that the feeling of Fear, instead of the truth of what we Fear, is the reason for the related uneasiness, stress, and despondency. At the point when we build up the propensity for boldness to make a move and steady self-assurance, an entirely different universe of conceivable outcomes opens up to us. Simply figure: What might you hope against hope, be, or do if you were not terrified of anything in the entire world?

Luckily, the habit of courage to take action could be learned, as it was when a local math teacher in Guinea powered his whole village. In Bolodou, a great many people were accustomed to utilizing battery-controlled lights around evening time. In any case, because of an aspiring venture by neighbourhood math educator Ibrahima Tounkara, the 90 family units in this little town in the south of Guinea have power every minute of every day. Tounkara sunk the majority of his savings into building a little dam. The thought satisfied, and the dam presently delivers 9 kW of intensity per day.

The strength to act can be learned. To do this, we must get down to business efficiently to decrease and destroy our feelings of fear while, at the same time, constructing the sort of mental fortitude that will empower us to manage the inescapable bad times of life.

In April 2017, residents of Treichville, a borough in Ivory Coast's capital Abidjan, had had enough of their dilapidated, dirty neighborhood. So, they pulled all their resources together and got to work slapping another coat of paint on each road, from the asphalts straight up to the overhang of houses. The undertaking was perceived by the government, and when it had been done, the Minister of Urban Hygiene Anne Ouloto and the country's first lady Dominique Ouattara came to the town to personally congratulate the workers.

We are all afraid, but how would you manage this emotion? A strong individual is essentially one who continues to act and move forward, regardless of the fear they feel.

What's more, here's something that I've realized: Face fearful feelings directly and push toward what you fear; your apprehensions will decrease, and your confidence and self-assurance will soar.

Be that as it may, when you stay away from the things that you fear, your feelings of fear mount until they start to control your life. What's more, as your feelings of trepidation become greater, your confidence, your self-assurance, and your sense of pride take a nosedive. People who are paralyzed by the fear of disappointing themselves or others spend way too much time covering or justifying their errors. Furthermore, some people are so afraid that others will reject them that they are incapable of acting without the approval of others.

As to your overwhelming apprehension, ask yourself these questions:

1. How does this fear keep me down throughout everyday life?

2. How does this fear assist me? How has it helped me previously?

3. What might happen if I conquer this fear?

A few years back, I took this questionnaire and reasoned that my greatest fear was the fear of neediness but poverty, in layman's terms. I feared not having enough cash, of being bankrupt, maybe even of being down and out.

My fear was strengthened when I was penniless on several different occasions at an early age. I could unbiasedly evaluate the source of that fear; however, despite everything, it continued to grip me. In any event, when I had adequate cash for every one of my needs, that fear remained consistently there.

My response to the inquiry "How does this fear keep me down throughout everyday life?" was that it made me fear going broke. It made risk-averse at work. Furthermore, it made me pick security over circumstances.

My response to the subsequent inquiry, "How does this fear assist me?" was that, to get away from the fear of destitution, I would, in general, work longer and harder than most people. I was goal-oriented and decisive. I put much more effort than most people into searching for different ways to earn money. The fear of destitution was, essentially, driving me toward financial independence.

At the point when I addressed the third question, "What might be my result for conquering this fear?" I promptly observed that I would go for more uncertainty that I would be more creative and assertive in my quest for financial security, I could and would go into business, and I would not be so tense and worried about spending excessively or having pretty much nothing. I would never again be worried about the cost of everything.

By unbiasedly examining my greatest fear along these lines, I could start conquering it. You can start to conquer your fear by engaging in activities that will increase your boldness and self-assurance. The future belongs to individuals who are risk-takers, not those who sit alone in their rooms. Sometimes in life, the more you look for security, the less of it you will have. But the more you look for circumstance, the more probable it is that you will accomplish the security that you want. Now, before you begin, here's an important point to remember: All intelligent people are afraid of something. Everyone worries about their health, their love lives, and whether they have enough money. Even bold, strong individuals experience fear. As Mark Twain stated, "Courage is protection from fear; it is the authority of fear, not the absence of fear."

The root of all fear is early childhood development, when we experience two kinds of fear: the fear of disappointment, which makes us figure, I can't, I can't, I can't; and the fear of rejection, which makes us think, I need to, I need to, I need to. The main way that you can circumvent these fears is to demonstrate to yourself incontrovertibly that it will be of greater benefit to you to act than to consider something once more. If you understand the benefits of activity, you will be more prepared to act when necessary. Here are just some of the benefits:

- Activity is cheaper than planning.

- Action allows emergence.

- Action is an existential answer.

- Action creates courage.

- Explanations follow actions.

There you have it; the main cure for stress is deliberate activity toward meeting an objective. When you plan how to resolve your concern, you won't have the opportunity or the psychological ability to stress. Also, before you know it, your troubling circumstance will have been settled. Conquering fear and acquiring the courage to make a move are basic requirements for a cheerful, fruitful life.

CHAPTER 11
THE IMPORTANCE OF TAKING DECISIVEACTION

Have you ever noticed how successful people just seem to fall on great opportunities? They always seem well-placed to achieve their objectives. We often think of them as lucky, but are they? It's actually about their ability to deliberate, and then take decisive action to reach their goals. So, what are they doing differently than less successful people? Effective individuals don't impose limits on themselves. They don't go through all of the reasons why it is not the right time to start something new; rather, they know that there is no better time than the present to take advantage of the opportunities that are presented to them.

To achieve anything, you must act because Learning + Action = Result. If you make decisions critically and you apply persistent, positive action, you will achieve desired outcomes more quickly. Even the smallest of positive actions in your life can bring about intense, positive changes that can improve each part of your life. To improve the quality of your activity, you have to improve your conviction; when your conviction increases, make positive changes. When you believe in the changes that you are making, you will obtain a positive outcome.

Knowing is not enough; we must apply what we learn. To be willing is not enough; we must act. In the long run, we will reap the benefits. Here are some powerful benefits to acting at the right time, at the right place, with the right person, for the right purpose.

1. Actions Put Your Knowledge into Practice

If you read any book or any inspirational article and glean knowledge from it, do you think that knowledge will completely change you? Not until you utilize that knowledge and learning; it is only when you act on that knowledge that your newly-acquired data can transform you. Reading books can provide you with tips, but you need to indulge in positive action in order to bring about change in your life.

For instance, suppose that you acquire some information with regards to business or housing; however, as opposed to utilizing that information toward your prosperity, you conceal this data from the world and remain alone in your home, doing nothing. If you do that, then what you have learned won't work for you; rather, use that information to decide on a truly inspired course of action.

2. Actions Help You to Achieve Your Goals

Reading books will permit you to learn new things, which will make you a more intelligent individual and, furthermore, give you a clearer picture of how to achieve your goals and make your dreams come true. Each goal can be broken down into a series of smaller actions, which are based on the knowledge that you have learned. This series of actions will, in addition to providing you with a growing sense of achievement, help you to achieve your goals.

3. Actions Provide Fulfilment

Suppose you go to a café and you have trouble selecting which cookie to purchase. Should you purchase the cookie that you normally buy, or should you purchase another type of cookie? Various thoughts might run through your head, such as: Will I like this new cookie? Will I like it more than the other cookie? What if this cookie is more expensive? What if I am allergic to this cookie? The point here is that if you stand there for a half-hour, trying to decide which cookie to buy, several different scenarios could occur. For example, they may run out of both types of cookies. That would be extremely unsatisfying. You could irritate the people who are standing in line behind you. You would probably become very hungry after about fifteen minutes of this indecision. It is only by deciding which cookie that you would like to buy that you will receive the reward for your deliberations: the cookie.

4. Consistent Action Becomes a Habit That Puts You on the Fast Track to Success

Taking action on one day, or over the course of a couple of days, won't bring about any genuine change in your life. Making positive changes and achieving things in your life is a process, and only one day of activity won't make any significant change in your life; consequently, in the event that you need to exchange your bad habits for better ones, you must make a move daily, over a prolonged period of time. For example, let's say that you need to start exercising; at that point, one day of aerobics will not only help you to stay fit. You need to make a move regularly; you need to exercise daily. Only then will you start to see a difference in your life.

5. Actions Dispel Confusion

You will never realize what procedures and/or tips do and don't work for you if you never take action. In the course of taking action, you will receive feedback as to which activities do and don't work for you; this process of trial and error will provide you with everything that you will need to make lasting, positive changes in your life.

6. The Three Rules for Taking Action

Moving ahead, so you've recognized the significance of making a move. At that point, what should you do? Regardless of what you've been attempting to accomplish, there are three general rules that you must follow in order to ensure your success:

Determine what you must make a move on: What parts of your life do you have to make changes to? Do you find that your mornings are not productive enough? Do you need to exercise more, or incorporate more healthy foods into your diet? Do you need to update your skills by taking a class at your local university?

Determine what essential actions you should take: Now that you have decided what element of your life that you wish to change, you are ready to determine what actions you should take. At this point, you must discard any impulsive or poorly-constructed courses of action. The remaining alternatives should be those which, after much deliberation, you have determined essential to your success. You may end up with a surplus of viable alternatives. Congrats! Now you have the freedom to adjust your course of action should external factors arise that could impact your first action plan.

CHAPTER 12
REASONS FOR INACTION AND
HOW TO ELIMINATE THEM

Positive reasoning, examination, reading comprehension, and attending online courses are all great contributors to success; however, none of these things will ever become a substitute for taking action. Being proactive is the way to progress.

There is no higher need than being proactive. The longer that a thought sits in your mind without being followed upon, the more useless it becomes. After seven days, it will be totally overlooked and will probably never be truly addressed again. So, what is stopping you from implementing that idea?

I was well into my 20s when I reflected on this question; I had just moved into a crisply-painted one-room loft. It was my first "solo" involvement – no flat mates, no pooch, and no guardians, and, though I am not an orphan, no kin. I could leave my messy socks on the lounge area table and stay up late playing my FIFA 19. I delighted in the opportunity of my isolation. Around three weeks after the fact, I was making myself supper when I understood that I was totally out of dishes – all of the plates and bowls were heaped in the sink. They had been standing by persistently, for a long while, to be washed.

So, I did what any self-regarding youthful lone ranger would do: I dashed over to the nearby store to purchase paper plates. Why those dishes hadn't been washed was a mystery, especially given the proximity of a well-working dishwasher that consumed a little space under the counter not a long way from the sink. Be that as it may, I never figured out how to get the dishwasher to reach over, get the dishes and turn itself on.

Admittedly, my necessary job in this procedure, while basic, was constrained. It didn't require extraordinary competence or knowledge. The assignment was not especially mind-boggling. The time required was negligible. So, what shielded me from making a move, from doing what should have been finished? Most of the explanations behind stalling all these activities have to do with emotional blockages like dread, tension, hesitation, hair splitting, and so on. I consider these boundaries the *"evil of inaction"* on account of Shoma Mirota, who created that terminology.

1. **You are frightened of jumpstarting out from your protected and secure spot.**

One of the most common obstacles to getting things done is fear. Strong emotions build up inside us. We start to worry. We start to envision all kinds of negative scenarios: disappointment, shame, dismissal, uneasiness, torment, and even death. As we become overwhelmed by our emotions, we may become frozen in inaction. We have every reason to be scared. What we think is a great idea, in theory, might prove not to be the case when tested in the real world.

The uplifting news for you is that you don't have to leave your protected activity to adopt new thoughts. You can begin little by little. Develop your intuition before dawn and work independently to test your thoughts. Put your spare time to valuable use by taking action to carry out your ideas. As you see the positive outcomes, you will grow in confidence. You will have the boldness to spend more time in the development and implementation of your ideas.

2. You don't need to be experienced or knowledgeable to carry out your idea.

At the click of a mouse, a vast reservoir of knowledge is available. There are numerous other resources as well: online communities, trade shows, and various other online ways that you can check out your competitors.

You don't need to redo someone else's research. Numerous others have done what you need to do. So, go out and discover them; learn from their knowledge. They might be too anxious to even think about talking about their encounters.

You can also seek out some books and courses if you require additional information. You will also need to strengthen your courage in order to acton your thoughts. Here are a couple of things you can do:

- Break down your huge thoughts into smaller chunks.

- Start by creating a list of the things that you need to do and check them off your list. Make a phone call, visit a competitor's site, or attend a trade show; you don't need to be experienced to accomplish something.

- Gain experience by taking action. You gain experience from the actions that you take, so don't delay getting that experience.

3. You don't need to have perfect timing.

Indeed, timing can be an important part of your success. But still, most of the time, it is only with the benefit of hindsight that you will realize that your idea was perfectly timed.

So, here is a simple solution. Figure out what it is that you would like to achieve, and then do it. Be adaptable and flexible. Be prepared to change course as more data becomes accessible.

If things don't turn out the way that you planned, be prepared to change course. Should you make fundamental changes to your plan now or wait until you have carried out the entire plan and conduct a post-mortem? The best time to make your move is now; there will never be an ideal time.

4. Do not take on so much that you become overwhelmed by your workload.

If you find that you become way too busy, you will not be able to take on new activities or new clients, and you will not be able to learn new skills.

There was a period in my life when things were not going well. My days were filled with crisis after crisis. There was no time to plan, no time to think, and no time to add to my skill set. I needed to make sense of why I was so occupied, yet I couldn't discover an opportunity to do it.

Ask yourself the following questions: Is what I am doing at this moment the best use of my time? What does my day cost? If I paid myself, what amount would I pay for an hour's work?

When I started to put a price tag on my time, I understood what to quit doing, what to designate, and what to reevaluate. So, I made some changes to what I was doing and divided my workload into more manageable pieces so that I could delegate it.

We have only 24hours in a day, and there is not a lot to do within this time because something will always come up. So, you need to manage your personal resources by building time management skills.

What you don't do is as significant as what you do.

- Develop your daily schedule; reevaluate it constantly.

- Delegate, delegate, delegate when it is necessary.

I have come to realize that, apart from a few individuals who can entirely self-motivate, by far, most of us need to have the right individuals around us to encourage, inspire, and motivate us to take action.

That's why motivational speakers get paid a lot of money to give speeches and say things everyone knows about but does nothing. But you can improve the likelihood of your progress by finding a mentor or friend (an accountability partner) to help keep you accountable and on track.

CHAPTER 13
BUILDING NEW HABITS: EXERCISE

Resolving to exercise is a constant struggle. For the first month, we devote ourselves entirely to our New Year's Resolutions to get to the gym every day or take a cardio class; then, we stop after a couple of days, weeks, or months because we simply don't possess the energy for it.

Throughout the years, I've come to understand that exercise isn't something that we feel motivated to set aside time for; instead, we have to set a goal that motivates us to find time in our daily schedule. Much the same as how we brush our teeth at the beginning of each day, exercise can be simply become something that we do every day out of habit. So how might we make exercise as regular as brushing our teeth?

Here are some excellent tips that will allow you to form new habits, such as exercising every day:

1. Take Small Steps

Have you ever promised yourself to work out daily for an hour, just to wind up back where you started from: in front of your television set, eating a large bag of potato chips? It might be because you tried to make too great change all at once. Make your exercise routine so natural and so easy to do that you can't think of a reason not to do it. For instance, as opposed to working out for an hour, simply practice for just 15 minutes, or start with only ten pushups per day. Shrinking the change causes you to stack up some speedy successes, which will eliminate your fear of failure and start you on the right track to achieving your exercise habits.

For example, take someone who wants to lose 250 pounds of weight but grew up on fried chicken and Hamburger Helper and spends most evenings vegetating on the couch. His eating habits have never improved, and his home is now loaded up with sweet treats and saltines, pizza, frozen yogurt, and gallons of pop. He realizes that acquiring new habits might be troublesome, so he confides in an advisor who has helped him previously on a number of occasions.

She reveals to him that the best way to change his eating habits is to eliminate his bad habits and acquire newer, better ones. He realizes that she is correct. He chooses to make little, manageable changes to his eating routine. He begins by removing only three junk foods: pizza, cheddar, and frozen yogurt. He tells himself that he can eat any other foods, just not those foods.

Gradually, he makes other changes. He swaps out pasta and rice with freekeh, a whole grain with loads of protein and fiber. The positive results are slow but steady. Almost every week, he loses a pound or two, and that keeps him motivated. By the spring of 2007, he has lost 30 pounds.

2. Create a cue and use it to trigger your habit.

A trigger is a cue, physical or not, that prods you to do a specific activity. For instance, placing your running shoes directly in front of your entryway may remind you to keep running for 10 minutes at the beginning of each day; an evening instant message from a companion may remind you to drop and complete 10 pushups. The best sorts of triggers are things that you, as of now, manage without deduction; things like heading off to the washroom toward the beginning of the day or brushing your teeth, function admirably as triggers.

3. Train the cycle and uplift

Habits take time to establish. Some specialists state that habits take a month to develop; others claim that it takes more time than that. Truly, it doesn't make a difference how long it takes; simply keep on doing the activity until you don't have to think about it anymore. When you hit this zone, start increasing the difficulty, for instance, by including an additional mile, or 20 additional pushups.

In addition to increasing the difficulty of your exercise routine by slow, incremental levels, you can add a greater variety of elements to your exercise plan. For example, Cristiano Ronaldo's training philosophy is to work out up to four hours per day, five days a week. Moreover, he eats up to six meals every day to make sure he has enough energy to train with the highest intensity possible and avoids alcoholic drinks as well, although before and during the games, he drinks CR7.

This strict eating routine, combined with his preparation, enables him to keep up an exceptionally low muscle mass (typically under 10 percent).

4. Shape Your Environment

There are many aspects to consider when shaping your environment. For example, you could overhaul your group of friends by surrounding yourself with individuals who exercise daily, or you could update your physical space by buying a disassembled up bar to trigger you to do five pull-ups a day consistently.

You could likewise include some form of reward to motivate yourself to maintain your healthy new habits, such as getting a massage or back rub on the weekend. Either way, it's essential to shape the conditions around you to make getting up and moving around as easy as could reasonably be expected. Changing any behavior into a habit requires mindful planning and patience; however, on the opposite side of all that is a feeling of accomplishment from establishing these healthy habits that can help you to feel joyful and proud.

When choosing which habits to create, be sure to review all of your options and their possible benefits. A happier, more productive life is yours for the taking. Remember: keep the change small, make a trigger, add repetition, and shape your environment, and you'll become healthier and get in shape.

CHAPTER 14
STEPS OF THE DECISION-MAKING PROCESS

Decision-making is a tool that comes in handy for virtually everyone, including business owners and leaders of all walks of life. It is also a process that takes various factors and elements into consideration to achieve predetermined objective. The decision-making process involves using a set of step-by-step procedures in which anyone can be sure to make a worthwhile decision based on the resources that are available to them to achieve their goals and aspirations.

Depending on the field of action, the decision-making process varies, but the following process can be used in your career or personal life. The right decision can prevent an impending disaster or correct an unfavorable situation. On the other hand, a poor decision can create logistical problems or even chaos.

Steps in the Decision-Making Process

Follow this process step-by-step in chronological order. By using your in-depth understanding of your problem or situation and these easy steps, you will be able to achieve the outcome you desire.

Step 1: Identify the decision to be made.

Step 2: Get relevant data.

Step 3: Examinepossible alternatives.

Step 4. Compare and contrast possible decisions based on constraints and possible consequences.

Step 5. Pick the most plausible decision.

Step 6. Take inspired action based on your decision.

Step 1: Identify the decision to be made: The first line of action in the decision-making process is to identify that there's a decision to be made, note the reasons to make such a decision, the specifics of the problem at hand, and possible solutions that the decision will bring to the table. This stage also involves deciphering the situation if it is a situation that demands urgent attention (decision) or one that requires attention in the future, thus determining the available time for the decision making the process. It is paramount to know when a decision ought to be made in order to avoid the possible consequences of indecision or the possibility that it may become too late to make a decision.

Step 2: Collect relevant data: This step involves

gathering relevant information about the subject matter. Even the smallest details may become important because in decision making, ignoring these vital bits of information may prove costly or disastrous. What you need are data, facts, and figures and, when making business decisions, especially those involving capital, you need statistical information and professional advice; all this falls under gathering relevant data.

Step 3: Examine possible alternatives: If you immediately have a clear picture of the situation based on the information at your disposal and a thorough personal understanding of the subject matter, then you can go ahead with creating a number of possible solutions to the problem at hand. Usually, there's more than one possible solution to a problem; document your progress (or failure) so that you can adjust quickly, if necessary, to changing conditions.

Step 4: Compare and contrast possible decisions based on your constraints: This stage is the point where you should begin to evaluate (compare and contrast) your alternatives based on their comparative feasibility, profit, and possible losses. List your constraints in order of preference and weigh your alternatives accordingly.

Step 5: Pick the most plausible decision: After completing Step 4, you will have established which decision is the most plausible. The most plausible decision is the one that proves most fruitful and worthwhile based on the available data and constraints at that particular point in time; it also produces the highest or desired output. Note that as things change and new information becomes available, you may need to remain flexible to achieve your desired outcome.

Step 6: Carry out the decision: This part is the very essence of the decision-making process, and the last step; at this stage, you should take inspired action. Based on your process, you should feel no dissonance at this critical stage. Stick to the plan and follow through using all the resources that you have available to you. You should have already gathered your resources by this point, as they would have assisted you in your decision-making process.

CHAPTER 15
TYPES OF DECISION-MAKING

There are many different types of decision making, and depending on subject matters, these decision-making approaches can be classified into a number of groups. These groups may include:

1. The Decision by Impulse

This type of decision-making is one of the most commonly employed types of decision-making; it relies solely on guts and intuition. A decision made using this method is not always the right one, but, in some cases, it is the best available option at that point in time. This type of decision-making doesn't rely on logic but is usually a product of the combination of what is present and the individual's intuition or guts.

Decisions in this category are usually be described using popular phrases, such as: 'I can feel it'; 'something is not right about all these'; 'I smell a rat', and so on. These decisions make use of what is called the 'sixth sense' or 'the third eye'. Although these methods have no scientific backing, history has shown that some people are blessed with the 'third eye' and can see what most people can't see, consequently making good decisions even in the most unsavory situations. In employing this method of decision-making, people pick up on certain information due to their strong intuition. It can be as simple as listening to their inner voice, and in extreme cases, individuals have reported seeing pictures or visions (sometimes through dreams) or just having a strong urge to take a certain action. Although these methods seem rather different, it is one of the most popular methods of decision-making used, especially in unfavorable situations.

2. Decision Made After Logical Reasoning

This is another method of decision-making that is also popular because even philosophy has asserted that all human beings are rational thinkers and so we use our thinking faculty, even during decision-making. This type of decision can also be called a rational decision; it is one that uses logic to consider all of the different sources of information that are available before going through with an action. This type of decision usually takes the pros and cons of each possible action into consideration and considers what will happen if each of the alternative courses of action is carried out or not carried out. The goal is to make a productive, sound, rational decision. This type of decision-making is used during academic research, market research, product development, and other fields of life.

3. Decision Made by Combining a Group of Decisions

This type of decision-making is one type of decision-making that we choose every day, sometimes even without realizing it. One example would be having mayonnaise and butter in your sandwich when the most popular option would be to pick just one of these condiments. This type of decision is a composite decision that encapsulates one or two sub decisions to achieve a common goal.

4. The Decision by the Scale of Preference

This is the simplest type of decision-making because it involves picking the alternative with the lowest odds of having a negative outcome. That is, you go with the action that gives you the least loss at that point in time, even if it does not necessarily bring you the most benefits as factors change. It is a logical decision, but it takes little or no time to go through with the action. A simple example is a little girl at the ice cream store with no idea about how the flavors taste; she has to make a decision on which flavor that she will buy; her decision-making style will be according to her scale of preference. What scale of preference would she use? She might use the scale of preference of the sizes (if they are in different sizes and the same price), but also, there will likely be two other scales of preference: one based on the color, and the other, on flavor.

5. Decision Made Only After Due Consultation

People have what they call a DIY (do it yourself) approach to achieving set objectives; however, this type of decision-making is the direct opposite of DIY. It's more like getting people to do your 'dirty' job (although it doesn't have to be a dirty job), and it can also involve a form of payment between the parties involved. An example is getting a PR firm to do market research for you or getting professional advice concerning a subject matter; this usually involves a form of payment for services rendered. An individual asking his or her friend for their opinion concerning an impending decision (even though it is for free) still falls under this type of decision making.

6. Decisions Made Based on Logic and Intuition

Getting a good bargain on anything requires achieving a balance between your intuitive and logical reasoning; this type of decision-making is very important for those who trust their research and yet still have a strong faith in their sixth sense, or what some people call their inner voice. This type of decision-making is a combination of decision-making types 1 and 2 that were discussed above.

The decision-making groups discussed above all have two important factors in common; these are Accountability and Productivity. Without these two factors, the decision will be less efficient in the long and short term.

Accountability: In decision-making, accountability basically means that the individual making the decisions is responsible for quality management, risk analysis, and desired results.

Productivity: Productivity means that a process is worthwhile, fruitful, and profitable under explicit and implicit constraints.

Productivity is essential because a mistake can decrease productivity, and cause the need to go through the decision-making process all over again.

How do I know if my decision is accountable and productive?

An accountable decision best considers the constraints and resources available; this decision ensures that the desired result or close enough to the desired result is achieved, and this can be repeated to achieve the same results, while a productive decision provides more output than it takes in input. In other words, productivity in decision making ensures 'profit' is made from the action taken, and in any case of loss increment, profit made is more than the loss incurred. Note: Profit and loss, as used in accountability and productivity, may not always be in financial terms. A productive decision brings little or no regrets. An accountable decision can always be trouble-shooted if necessary.

CONCLUSION

Wayne Gretzky once said, "You lose a hundred percent of the shots you don't take". Time is sometimes a luxury that you can't afford, and overthinking is a waste of our precious time. If you find yourself ruminating, experiencing an above-normal amount of fear and anxiety, and your thinking does not lead to inspired action, you are overthinking. In the short-term, overthinking can lead to anxiety, fear, and a lack of self-confidence. In the long-term, research has shown that overthinking can lead to dreaded ailments like high blood pressure, hypertension and, in worse cases, even death.

However, rational and critical thinking are essential, especially as all action or inaction has consequences, be they negative or positive. If you channel the energy that you spend while overthinking into action, you will be sure to achieve the results that you desire, if not immediately, then over the course of time and trial and error. In some cases, it may be better to risk making a mistake than to risk the result of inaction, but this is only to be advised when your potential errors can be reversed and do not lead to a loss of time or material resources.

Aside from the fact that taking action saves you from the mental stress of overthinking, it also channels your energy into something that will be more productive and rewarding for you. There are many different types of decision-making that you can use to make decisions; choose the one that works best for you and stick with it. There is no hard-and-fast rule for the amount of time that you should spend considering all possible scenarios before taking action. It is less about the amount of time that you spend and more about whether your thinking process remains logical and productive.

It is especially important to avoid overthinking in life or death situations. For example, a renowned brain surgeon, Dr. Ben Carson, was once was faced with a dire situation where he had to act quickly to save an accident victim, even though he was only a new resident doctor. However, despite the risk involved, he understood the importance of quickly deciding on a course of action; Dr. Ben Carson carried out the operation, and it was a successful one, thus marking the beginning of an illustrious career as a renowned brain surgeon. Had he been prone to overthinking, the patient would most certainly have died.

Even when the consequences of overthinking are much less dire, so many dreams remain dreams because the individuals with creative ideas and brilliant imaginations are too fearful or anxious from overthinking to put their dreams into practice. Without action, a work of art as tangible and beautiful as the world-famous Mona Lisa painting would not exist. History will forever celebrate people like Leonardo da Vinci for their countless contributions to the arts; they will also celebrate inventors like Paul Darwin or Michael Faraday. These individuals achieved great things through inspired action, not overthinking.

Action is necessary to put our most inspired thoughts and ideas into practice, to solve problems and resolve issues, and to live our productively and fully. Overthinking paralyzes us, preventing us from taking the very actions that will ensure our contentment, fulfilment, and survival. By overcoming overthinking and learning how to incorporate rational, critical thinking in our lives, we can put our most inspired ideas into action and leave a lasting mark on the world.